ZODIAC SIGNS

LEO

July 23 – August 22

Jennifer Howse

AV2

www.av2books.com

AV2

Step 1
Go to **www.av2books.com**

Step 2
Enter this unique code
BDLZEOBT2

Step 3
Explore your interactive eBook!

AV2 is optimized for use on any device

Your interactive eBook comes with...

Contents
Browse a live contents page to easily navigate through resources

Audio
Listen to sections of the book read aloud

Videos
Watch informative video clips

Weblinks
Gain additional information for research

Try This!
Complete activities and hands-on experiments

Key Words
Study vocabulary, and complete a matching word activity

Quizzes
Test your knowledge

Slideshows
View images and captions

... and much, much more!

ZODIAC SIGNS

LEO

July 23 – August 22

Contents

2 AV2 Book Code
4 Are You a Leo?
6 It's in the Stars
8 The Myth of Leo
10 Leo and Fixed Signs
12 Leo as a Fire Sign
14 Being a Leo
16 Leos through Time
18 Making Friends
20 Know Your Leos
22 The Leo Quiz
23 Key Words/Index

Are You a Leo?

Do people call you a good friend? Are you the life of the party? If this sounds familiar, you might be a Leo. A Leo is someone who was born between July 23 and August 22.

Leo is a sign in the zodiac. This is a series of 12 **constellations** that run across the night sky. For centuries, people have used these groups of stars to tell the future. The study of the stars in this manner is called astrology.

Zodiac Chart

A person's zodiac sign is determined by his or her date of birth. Which sign matches your birthday?

It's in the Stars

The zodiac constellations form a circle around Earth. In one year, Earth makes a full **orbit** around the Sun. As it does this, the Sun appears to be in different places at set times. The zodiac constellations are found along the path the Sun follows.

Long ago, people used the Sun to tell the time of year. In late July, the Sun passed through the Leo constellation. People born then were said to be born under the sign of Leo.

Over time, the position of the constellations shifted. Even though the Sun now passes through Leo at a different time, the dates associated with the sign of Leo remain the same.

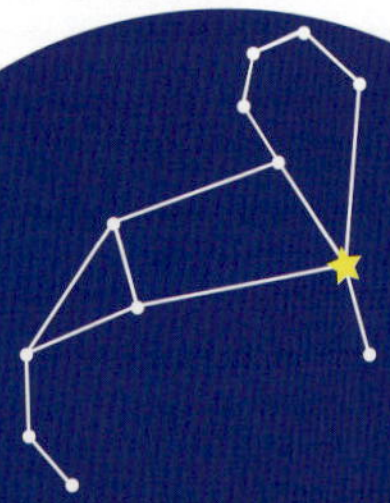

Leo's brightest point is called **Regulus**. It looks like a **single star**, but is actually **4 stars**.

Regulus radiates **360 times** the energy of the **Sun**.

Leo rises and sets at different times, depending on where in the world you observe it from.

The Myth of Leo

The ancient Greeks had stories about how each zodiac constellation came to be in the sky. Leo is linked to a monster called the Nemean lion.

The Nemean lion was a deadly creature. It was terrorizing the area of Nemea. A Greek hero named Heracles was charged with killing the lion. However, the lion had fur that could not be pierced by weapons, making it unstoppable.

At first, Heracles tried to shoot the lion with arrows, but they could not penetrate its legendary fur. So, he came up with a plan to trap the fearsome creature instead. Once the lion went inside its lair, Heracles blocked the exit so it could not escape. Then, Heracles entered the cave and strangled the beast with his bare hands.

Triumphant, Heracles placed the lion in the sky to display his **conquest**. Its image can still be seen in the night sky today as the constellation Leo.

Heracles was sent to complete 12 labors, or tasks. Killing the Nemean lion was the first of these labors.

Leo and Fixed Signs

In astrology, some zodiac signs share certain **qualities**. These qualities show how a person acts in the world. The qualities are separated into three groups. Cardinal signs are often action-oriented. Fixed signs like to share their ideas with others. Mutable signs use their knowledge to solve problems.

Leo is a fixed sign. People in this group are very focused. They are determined to finish whatever projects they start. Fixed signs are also reliable people. They can be trusted to be loyal friends.

Fixed signs like making the world a better place for everyone to live.

Zodiac Signs
by Quality

Cardinal Signs
Are often action-oriented.

Aries · Cancer · Libra · Capricorn

Fixed Signs
Like to share their ideas with others.

Taurus · Leo · Scorpio · Aquarius

Mutable Signs
Use their knowledge to solve problems.

Gemini · Virgo · Sagittarius · Pisces

Leo as a Fire Sign

Zodiac signs are also grouped according to the four **classical elements**. These are fire, earth, water, and air. Signs that belong to the same group share common personality traits.

Leo is a fire sign. Fire people have a great **zest** for life. They enjoy a variety of different activities. Fire people are typically sure of their ideas. They work hard to make their visions become reality.

Fire signs are known for being fun people to be around.

Zodiac Signs
by Element

Being a Leo

A Leo's fire traits and fixed qualities combine to create a specific type of person. A key Leo strength is **good humor**. Leos love to gather with friends. They are happiest when learning new things.

Leos have their weaknesses as well. They enjoy playing games and sports, but can be extremely competitive. This drive to win may cause rivalries to occur. Despite their competitive nature, Leos are also generous. They like to share in the fun when others win, too.

In **2020**, there were **20 billionaire Leos** around the world.

Leos are ruled by the Sun. Its **surface** can reach temperatures of up to **10,000 degrees Fahrenheit**. (5,500 degrees Celsius)

Leos prefer a small circle of close, supportive friends.

Leos through Time

Leos have had a significant impact on the world over time. They have written classic stories, set impressive records, and advanced our knowledge of the **universe**. Their contributions have helped make the world what it is today.

1804

Military leader **Napoleon Bonaparte** (born August 15, 1769) declares himself emperor of France.

1901

Writer **Beatrix Potter** (born July 28, 1866) publishes *The Tale of Peter Rabbit*, the first in her series of beloved children's books set in the English countryside.

1932

Aviator **Amelia Earhart** (born July 24, 1897) becomes the first female pilot to fly solo across the Atlantic Ocean.

1970s

Scientist **Vera Rubin** (born July 23, 1928) does research that will later lead to the discovery of **dark matter**.

2009

Civil rights lawyer **Barack Obama** (born August 4, 1961) becomes the first African American president of the United States.

2020

Professional tennis player **Roger Federer** (born August 8, 1981) becomes the world's highest-paid athlete, with earnings of $106.3 million.

Making Friends

Some people believe that zodiac signs can affect the way people get along with one another. Each sign has its own traits. These traits can be a good fit with other signs. A Leo might be drawn to certain people, based on their signs.

It's Friendship

Leos get along well with people born under these signs.

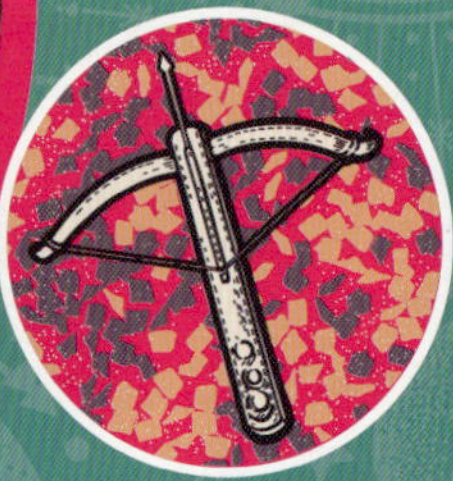

Sagittarius

Aries

Gemini

It's Love

Leos often find romance with these signs.

Aquarius

Gemini

Libra

It's Complicated

Leos find it difficult to form bonds with these signs.

Taurus

Capricorn

Scorpio

Know Your Leos

Leos continue to make an impact on the world. They can be found doing good work in various fields. Did you know these people are Leos?

J.K. Rowling

Born: July 31, 1965

J.K. (Jo) Rowling is best known as the creator of the Wizarding World. This magical franchise includes the Harry Potter book and film series, as well as the *Fantastic Beasts* film series. In addition to being a writer, Jo is a **philanthropist**. She founded Lumos, a charity that helps children in orphanages around the world.

Actor Daniel Radcliffe played Harry Potter in the films. Both Daniel and Harry are Leos like Jo.

Rico Rodriguez

Born: July 31, 1998

Actor Rico Rodriguez first rose to fame on the sitcom *Modern Family*. He has appeared on the big screen as well, in *The Muppets*. Rico also supports the Head Start Program, which provides disadvantaged children with education and nutrition.

Tom Brady

Born: August 3, 1977

Professional football player Tom Brady is a star quarterback in the National Football League (NFL). He holds the record for the player with the most **Super Bowl** wins. Tom supports many charities as well, including Best Buddies, which creates opportunities for people with disabilities.

Shawn Mendes

Born: August 8, 1988

Shawn Mendes is an award-winning singer and songwriter. His first single, "Life of the Party," was released in 2014. Since then, he has had several Top Ten hits. Shawn plays both piano and guitar. He also heads a foundation that supports and helps children.

Anna Kendrick

Born: August 9, 1985

Actress and singer Anna Kendrick started her career as a child on **Broadway**. She has starred in the popular *Twilight* and *Pitch Perfect* film franchises. Anna also voiced the character Poppy in the animated film *Trolls* and its sequel, *Trolls World Tour*.

The Leo QUIZ

1 Which historical Leo declared himself emperor of France in 1804?

2 What is the brightest point in the constellation Leo?

3 Which object in the solar system rules Leo?

4 Who defeated the Nemean lion?

5 To which element group do Leos belong?

6 Which celebrity Leo is famous for creating the Wizarding World?

7 What zodiac signs make good friends for Leos?

8 Which Leo was the first female pilot to fly solo across the Atlantic Ocean?

ANSWERS: 1. Napoleon Bonaparte 2. Regulus 3. The Sun 4. Heracles
5. Fire 6. J.K. Rowling 7. Sagittarius, Aries, and Gemini 8. Amelia Earhart

Key Words

Broadway: an area of New York City, where there are many theaters

classical elements: materials from which all other materials were once believed to be made

conquest: something that has been successfully conquered or defeated

constellations: groups of stars that form patterns in the sky

dark matter: materials that cannot be directly seen or observed

good humor: cheerful or positive mood or disposition

orbit: a regular, repeating path that one object in space takes around another

philanthropist: someone who promotes the welfare of others

qualities: traits that make something what it is

Super Bowl: the annual championship game of the NFL

universe: everything that exists in space

zest: enthusiasm or energy

Index

astrology 4, 10

Bonaparte, Napoleon 16, 22
Brady, Tom 21

cardinal signs 10, 11
constellations 4, 6, 8, 22

Earhart, Amelia 17, 22
elements 12, 13, 22

Federer, Roger 17
fixed signs 10, 11, 14

Heracles 8, 9, 22

Kendrick, Anna 21

Mendes, Shawn 21
mutable signs 10, 11
myth 8

Nemean lion 8, 9, 22

Obama, Barack 17

Potter, Beatrix 16

qualities 10, 11, 14

Radcliffe, Daniel 20
Rodriguez, Rico 21
Rowling, J.K. 20, 22
Rubin, Vera 17

traits 12, 14, 18

zodiac 4, 5, 6, 8, 10, 11, 12, 13, 18, 22

Get the best of both worlds.

AV2 bridges the gap between print and digital.

The expandable resources toolbar enables quick access to content including **videos**, **audio**, **activities**, **weblinks**, **slideshows**, **quizzes**, and **key words**.

Animated videos make static images come alive.

Resource icons on each page help readers to further **explore key concepts**.

Published by AV2
14 Penn Plaza 9th Floor
New York, NY 10122
Website: www.av2books.com

Library of Congress Control Number: 2020938551

ISBN 978-1-7911-2632-2 (hardcover)
ISBN 978-1-7911-2633-9 (softcover)
ISBN 978-1-7911-2634-6 (multi-user eBook)
ISBN 978-1-7911-2635-3 (single-user eBook)

Printed in Guangzhou, China
1 2 3 4 5 6 7 8 9 0 24 23 22 21 20

062020
101119

Editor: Katie Gillespie
Art Director: Terry Paulhus

Every reasonable effort has been made to trace ownership and to obtain permission to reprint copyright material. The publisher would be pleased to have any errors or omissions brought to their attention so that they may be corrected in subsequent printings.

AV2 acknowledges Getty Images, Alamy, iStock, Shutterstock, and Dreamstime as its primary image suppliers for this title.